Hidden Gems

Practical Wisdom from the Prophet of Islam

Hidden Gems

Practical Wisdom from the Prophet of Islam

Compilation & Commentary:

MUSTAFA UMAR

HIDDEN GEMS

Copyright © 2013 by *Mustafa Umar*

Fourth Edition

ISBN-13: 978-1481878586

ISBN-10: 1481878581

www.mustafaumar.com

Printed in the United States of America

In the Name of God
The Most Kind and Merciful

CONTENTS

Introduction 9

ITEM 1: *Build Good Habits* 11

ITEM 2: *Excel in Everything You Do* 12

ITEM 3: *Maintain Good Conduct* 13

ITEM 4: *Don't Overfill Your Stomach* 14

ITEM 5: *Don't Criticize Food* 15

ITEM 6: *Beware of Extravagance & Rrogance* 16

ITEM 7: *Don't Be a Slave to Money* 17

ITEM 8: *Fear Excessive Luxury* 18

ITEM 9: *Wealth is a Test* 19

ITEM 10: *Appreciate What You Have* 20

ITEM 11: *True Wealth is Contentment* 21

ITEM 12: *Choose Your Friends Carefully* 22

ITEM 13: *Don't Be Selfish* 23

ITEM 14: *Be Sincere in Deeds* 24

ITEM 15: *Guide Others to Good* 25

ITEM 16: *Create Positive Change* 26

ITEM 17: *Control Your Anger* 27

ITEM 18: *Avoid the Irrelevant* 28

GEM 19:	*Watch Your Tongue*	29
GEM 20:	*Don't Laugh Excessively*	30
GEM 21:	*Don't Forget God*	31
GEM 22:	*Don't Speak Ill of Others*	32
GEM 23:	*Give Others the Benefit of the Doubt*	33
GEM 24:	*Think Before You Speak*	34
GEM 25:	*Learn From Your Mistakes*	35
GEM 26:	*Seize the Day*	36
GEM 27:	*What Goes Around Comes Around*	3
GEM 28:	*Don't Exaggerate*	3
GEM 29:	*Do Your Part*	3
GEM 30:	*What's Done is Done*	4
GEM 31:	*The Highest Level of Worship*	4
GEM 32:	*Life is a Test*	4
GEM 33:	*The Believer Never Loses*	4
GEM 34:	*True Wisdom is to Prepare for Death*	4
GEM 35:	*Life is a Journey*	4
GEM 36:	*It's What's Inside That Counts*	4
GEM 37:	*True Superiority is in Piety*	4
GEM 38:	*Cleanliness Counts*	4
GEM 39:	*The Natural Religion*	4
GEM 40:	*The Insignificance of This World*	5

his booklet is a selection of the sayings of Muhammad, the last Messenger of God sent to guide mankind.

he wisdom of a Prophet is not like that of any other man. It is revealed by the All Wise and All Knowing, while human thoughts are confined by the limitations of the intellect.

very saying in this booklet has been selected with the following considerations:

* Usefulness in everyday life
* Straightforwardness
* Brevity
* Ability to be easily memorized and referenced

these brief words of wisdom provide solutions to common problems that frequently occur throughout life.

therefore, it is recommended that the meanings be memorized, if possible, or at least kept nearby for reference purposes.

9

A brief explanation follows each saying in order to:

- ◆ Restate the point of wisdom in different words
- ◆ Extract other lessons that may not be directly apparent upon a casual reading

All sayings are authentically attributed to the Prophet and references to the sources are provided with the Arabic text.

May God allow us to benefit from these timeless gems of wisdom.

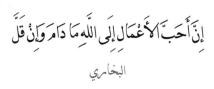

إِنَّ أَحَبَّ الأَعْمَالِ إِلَى اللَّهِ مَا دَامَ وَإِنْ قَلَّ

البخاري

The most beloved actions to God are those performed consistently, even if they are few.

Although impulsive good deeds are beneficial, actions performed consistently are better because they require more self-control, discipline, and commitment to God.

God has prescribed excellence in everything you do.

All actions, even seemingly insignificant ones, should be performed completely and properly.

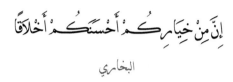

إِنَّ مِنْ خِيَارِكُمْ أَحْسَنَكُمْ أَخْلَاقًا

البخاري

The best of you have the best conduct.

Behave properly, because good conduct is a measure of inward excellence.

مَا مَلأَ آدَمِيٌّ وِعَاءً شَرًّا مِنْ بَطْنٍ بِحَسْبِ ابْنِ آدَمَ أُكُلاَتٌ
يُقِمْنَ صُلْبَهُ فَإِنْ كَانَ لاَ مَحَالَةَ فَثُلُثٌ لِطَعَامِهِ وَثُلُثٌ
لِشَرَابِهِ وَثُلُثٌ لِنَفْسِهِ

الترمذي وصحّحه

A man doesn't fill any vessel worse than his own stomach. Small meals that keep the back straight are sufficient. If that isn't possible then keep a third for food, a third for drink, and a third for space to breathe.

An amount of food that is enough to keep the body healthy is sufficient. Refrain from overeating because it is unhealthy and leads to many other problems.

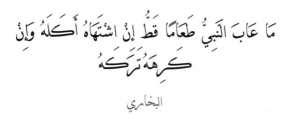

البخاري

The Prophet never criticized any food. If he liked something he ate it and if he disliked it he left it for others.

Different people naturally have different tastes. However, there is no need to complain if you don't get what you want.

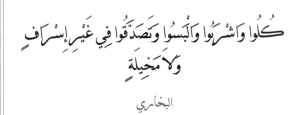

كُلُوا وَاشْرَبُوا وَالْبَسُوا وَتَصَدَّقُوا فِي غَيْرِ إِسْرَافٍ وَلاَ مَخِيلَةٍ

البخاري

Eat, drink, dress, and spend, with neither extravagance nor arrogance.

Extravagance is wastefulness while arrogance blinds from the truth.

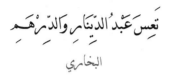

Cursed is the slave of gold and silver.

❁ ❁ ❁

Money has an inherent attraction that can enslave people and ruin their lives. Don't live in pursuit of wealth.

لَا الْفَقْرَ أَخْشَى عَلَيْكُمْ وَلَكِنْ أَخْشَى
عَلَيْكُمْ أَنْ تُبْسَطَ عَلَيْكُمُ الدُّنْيَا كَمَا بُسِطَتْ
عَلَى مَنْ كَانَ قَبْلَكُمْ فَتَنَافَسُوهَا كَمَا تَنَافَسُوهَا
وَتُهْلِكُكُمْ كَمَا أَهْلَكَتْهُمْ

البخاري

Poverty is not what I fear for you. Rather, I fear
that the world will open up its treasures for you
the way it opened up for those before you. You
will compete for it the way they competed for it
and it will destroy you the way it destroyed them.

Prosperity has the ability to cause even more problems than poverty. One must learn from the past
and be careful not to fall into the same trap that
others once fell into.

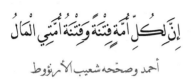

Every community has had a test. The test of my community will be wealth.

Wealth is a blessing from God that has been loaned to every individual. They will be held accountable on the Day of Judgment as to how they used it.

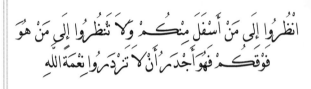

انْظُرُوا إِلَى مَنْ أَسْفَلَ مِنْكُمْ وَلاَ تَنْظُرُوا إِلَى مَنْ هُوَ
فَوْقَكُمْ فَهُوَ أَجْدَرُ أَنْ لاَ تَزْدَرُوا نِعْمَةَ اللهِ

مسلم

Look at those people who are less fortunate than you, not at those who are more fortunate than you so that you do not belittle the blessings of God upon you.

Everyone has been given different blessings such as health, wealth, beauty, or intelligence and must be thankful for what they have. Place yourself in proper perspective relative to others so that you will be thankful.

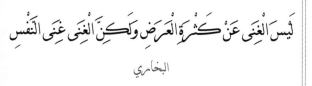

Prosperity should not be measured by material possessions. True wealth is contentment of the heart.

Money cannot buy happiness. True satisfaction lies in being satisfied with what you have.

الرَّجُلُ عَلَى دِينِ خَلِيلِهِ فَلْيَنْظُرْ أَحَدُكُمْ مَنْ يُخَالِلُ

البخاري

A person follows the path of his friends, so be careful whom you befriend.

Your companions have a strong ability to influence the way you think and behave, so be careful when choosing them.

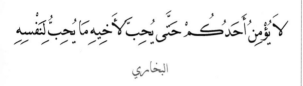

البخاري

None of you truly believes until he loves for his brother what he loves for himself.

Be selfless and want for others what you would want for yourself.

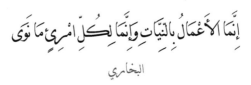

البخاري

Deeds are based upon their intentions and every person will be rewarded according to what he intended.

God knows what is in the hearts and will judge the sincerity of an action rather than its outward manifestation.

Whoever guides towards a good action receives the same reward as its performer.

Encouraging others towards a good deed is so great that it is as though you did the deed yourself.

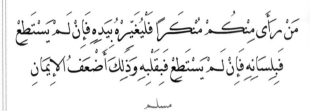

Whoever sees something bad should correct it with his hand. If one is unable to then with his tongue. If still unable then he should at least hate it in his heart. This is the weakest level of faith.

If you see something wrong don't just sit there, fix it! If unable to do so, then at least know that it is wrong and hate it in your heart.

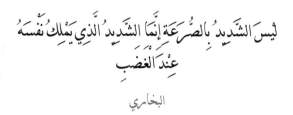

البخاري

The strong one is not the expert fighter. The truly strong is he who controls himself when angry.

The real measure of strength is not mere muscle, but rather self-control.

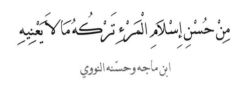

It's better for a Muslim to leave what doesn't concern him.

Don't waste time with matters that don't concern you, especially other peoples' affairs, because there are many other important things that require your attention.

البخاري

Whoever believes in God and the Hereafter should say something good or keep quiet.

If you have nothing beneficial to say then it is better to not say anything at all.

لَا تُكْثِرُوا الضَّحِكَ فَإِنَّ كَثْرَةَ الضَّحِكِ تُمِيتُ الْقَلْبَ

ابن ماجه وصححه الألباني

Don't laugh too much because excessive laughter
kills the heart.

Excessive joking and entertainment might make
you heedless of the meaning and purpose of life.

Don't speak too much without remembering God because this hardens the heart. Indeed, the furthest from God are the hard-hearted.

❁ ❁ ❁

Excessive speech or thought without the remembrance of God causes heedlessness. The mind remains conscious of what it constantly remembers.

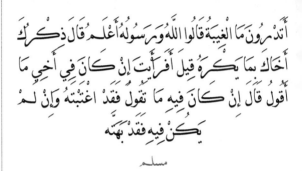

The Prophet asked, "Do you know what backbiting is?" They replied, "God and His Messenger know best." He said, "It is to mention something about another in his absence that he would dislike."

The Prophet was then asked, "What if I speak the truth about him?"

He then replied, "If you speak the truth then you are backbiting and if you lie then you are slandering"

Don't speak ill of anyone in his absence even if it is true, unless it is necessary for a legitimate reason

32

Be careful of forming bad opinions about others. Unjustified accusations are among the most un-truthful forms of speech.

Give others the benefit of the doubt and do not assume bad things about them since you would want the same for yourself.

It is enough of a lie to repeat everything one hears.

❁ ❁ ❁

Confirm what you hear so that you don't end up spreading rumors and false information.

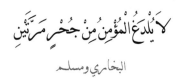

A believer is not stung from the same hole twice.

Everyone makes mistakes, but the key is to learn lessons from them and to avoid repeating them.

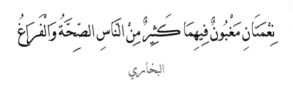

البخاري

Two blessings which many people waste are health and free time.

Take advantage of health before sickness and free time before busyness.

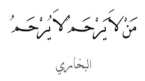

Whoever does not show mercy to others will not be shown mercy.

❀ ❀ ❀

God is just and will not show mercy on the Day of Judgment to those who did not show mercy to others during their lifetimes.

Exaggeration is destruction.

❀ ❀ ❀

Don't exaggerate beyond the limits in speech or actions.

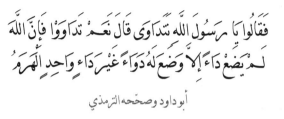

فَقَالُوا يَا رَسُولَ اللَّهِ نَتَدَاوَى قَالَ نَعَمْ تَدَاوَوْا فَإِنَّ اللَّهَ
لَمْ يَضَعْ دَاءً إِلاَّ وَضَعَ لَهُ دَوَاءً غَيْرَ دَاءٍ وَاحِدٍ الْهَرَمُ

أبو داود وصحّحه الترمذي

Some Companions asked, "Messenger of God, should we use medicine when sick?" The Prophet replied, "Yes, you may use medicine. God has not created any disease without also creating its cure, except old age."

Put your trust in God but do not abandon the means He created for you. Once you have taken the necessary steps, don't worry and leave the rest to God. This principle applies to all aspects of life.

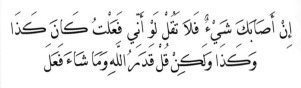

مسلم

If something happened to you don't say, "If only I hadn't done that, things would be different." Rather, say, "God decreed it and did whatever He wanted."

Never look back and regret the past. Feel sorry for what you did and only look back to learn lessons from your mistakes so you won't repeat them.

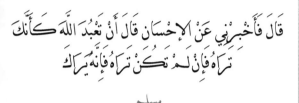

قَالَ فَأَخْبِرْنِي عَنِ الإِحْسَانِ قَالَ أَنْ تَعْبُدَ اللَّهَ كَأَنَّكَ تَرَاهُ فَإِنْ لَمْ تَكُنْ تَرَاهُ فَإِنَّهُ يَرَاكَ

مسلم

Someone said to the Prophet, "Inform me about sincerity." He replied, "Sincerity is to worship God as if you can see Him. Although you can't see Him, know that He sees you."

Strive to worship God with such devotion as if you are directly in His presence. Realizing that He sees you should help you perfect your worship.

This world is a prison for the believer and paradise for the non-believer.

❁ ❁ ❁

The believer, eagerly awaiting Paradise, feels trapped in this world, while the non-believer, unwilling to face death, sees this world and its enjoyments as Paradise.

عَجَبًا لِأَمْرِ الْمُؤْمِنِ إِنَّ أَمْرَهُ كُلَّهُ خَيْرٌ وَلَيْسَ ذَاكَ
لِأَحَدٍ إِلاَّ لِلْمُؤْمِنِ إِنْ أَصَابَتْهُ سَرَّاءُ شَكَرَ فَكَانَ
خَيْرًا لَهُ وَإِنْ أَصَابَتْهُ ضَرَّاءُ صَبَرَ فَكَانَ خَيْرًا لَهُ

مسلم

The life of a believer is truly amazing. Everything that happens to him is good. This is only true for a believer and none else. If something pleasant happens to him, he is thankful and that is good for him and if something bad afflicts him, he is patient and that is also good for him.

A believer is never overcome by difficulties. He re-alizes whatever happens is part of the greater test of life. The disbeliever denies this test and gains no benefit from afflictions.

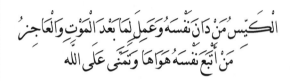

الْكَيِّسُ مَنْ دَانَ نَفْسَهُ وَعَمِلَ لِمَا بَعْدَ الْمَوْتِ وَالْعَاجِزُ
مَنْ أَتْبَعَ نَفْسَهُ هَوَاهَا وَتَمَنَّى عَلَى الله

الترمذي وحسنه

Wise is he who controls his desires and works for
the afterlife. Foolish is he who follows his desires
and then hopes God will forgive him.

True wisdom is to see life in perspective and overcome your desires in order to pass life's tests. Fool-
ishness is to hope that you will succeed without
making any effort.

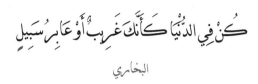

كُنْ فِي الدُّنْيَا كَأَنَّكَ غَرِيبٌ أَوْ عَابِرُ سَبِيلٍ

البخاري

Live in this world as if you are a stranger or a traveler.

A believer knows that he is only passing through this world and does not take it as his final destination. Like a traveler, he takes only what he needs and leaves behind that which will slow his journey.

45

IT'S WHAT'S INSIDE THAT COUNTS

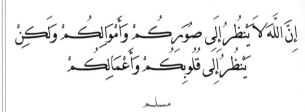

إِنَّ اللَّهَ لاَ يَنْظُرُ إِلَى صُوَرِكُمْ وَأَمْوَالِكُمْ وَلَكِنْ يَنْظُرُ إِلَى قُلُوبِكُمْ وَأَعْمَالِكُمْ

مسلم

God doesn't look at your appearances or your wealth. He looks at your hearts and your actions.

Outward appearances, empty deeds, and material possessions do not matter to God. Only sincere deeds really matter.

46

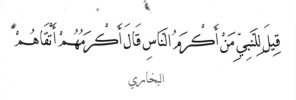

قِيلَ لِلنَّبِيِّ مَنْ أَكْرَمُ النَّاسِ قَالَ أَكْرَمُهُمْ أَتْقَاهُمْ

البخاري

It was said to the Prophet, "Who are the best people?" He replied, "The best of them are the most God-conscious."

Your rank is not determined by your lineage, race, or wealth, but rather by how mindful of God you are in your heart and actions.

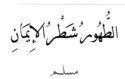

Cleanliness is half of faith.

Keeping yourself and your surroundings clean has been compared with being half of faith. Strive for cleanliness even if no one else can see it.

مَا مِنْ مَوْلُودٍ إِلاَّ يُولَدُ عَلَى الْفِطْرَةِ فَأَبَوَاهُ يُهَوِّدَانِهِ أَوْ
يُنَصِّرَانِهِ أَوْ يُمَجِّسَانِهِ

مسلم

Every child is born with a natural disposition towards the truth but his parents then make him a Jew, a Christian, or a fire worshipper.

All people have a natural inclination to believe in one God and accept His true religion, but external influences divert them and lead them astray.

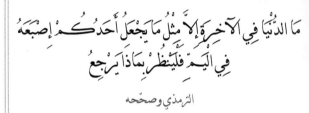

مَا الدُّنْيَا فِي الْآخِرَةِ إِلَّا مِثْلُ مَا يَجْعَلُ أَحَدُكُمْ إِصْبَعَهُ فِي الْيَمِّ فَلْيَنْظُرْ بِمَاذَا يَرْجِعُ

الترمذي وصحّحه

This world compared with the Hereafter is nothing more than a drop in an ocean.

This worldly life is virtually insignificant in every aspect when compared with the Hereafter. Never prefer this world over the Hereafter.

For more information, please visit our website at:

www.mustafaumar.com

Made in the USA
Middletown, DE
10 February 2023

24457632R00033